BREAKING THE SILENCE
&
SHOUTING FOR JOY

MARVIE BOLAND

Breaking The Silence & Shouting for Joy Copyright © December 2016 by Marvie Boland

Published in the United States of America by
Gospel 4 U Network

www.gospel4unetwork.com

All rights reserved. No part of this book may be reproduced or transmitted in anyway by means, electronic, mechanical, Photocopy, recording or otherwise, without prior permission of the author except as provided by USA copyright law.

Scriptures are taken from the
Holy Bible unless otherwise marked.
ISBN - 978-0-9984665-0-7
Library of Congress Number – 2016962586
Printed in United States of America
December 2016

Content

FOREWORD

DEDICATION

ACKNOWLEDGEMENT

INTRODUCTION

A Grandmother's Touch 13

Voices in the wind 19

Peace, Love & Nature 23

Listening in the silence 27

Paint my life with bright colors
and beautiful people 31

Why are you so unhappy that you are crying........ 35

Cold wind had the power to rule 39

Busta: Backbone of the Family 45

Raven and my Grandmother 51

I am the Woman living over there 57

WORDS OF ENCOURAGEMENTS 63

DAILY DECLARATIONS 85

MARVIE BOLAND

Foreword

There are certain days in your life you consider lucky ones. One that is know was so extremely lucky for me was the day that Marvie Boland came into mine.

I was a month away from giving birth to my fourth child. I was looking for someone to help me get organized. In a few short weeks I knew that more chaos would be coming at me in full force. Conversations with Shelly Gowan and Paula Singer reassured me that I met someone who would be just that person. Someone who helped them raise their children into the amazing people they are today.

Marvie quickly became my fast friend, confidante, teacher and mentor.

Marvie has had an incredible life filled with challenges and many, many blessings. From the day she was born as a premature infant her grandmother gave her the name "Marvelous Marvie" and she proves that to all that know her everyday.

I always tell Marvie that everything she touches becomes beautiful. From her clothing designs, interior decorating, cooking...I could go on and on. She never ceases to amaze me.

Marvie and Buster have a true fairytale marriage. They are great role models for their six fantastic children and -grandchildren.

To those of you who are lucky enough to be reading this book I know you will learn about the wonderful person I have come to know.

I cannot tell you how touched and honored I am to be writing this forward to your life story.

You will forever be a member of my family. You mean the world to me, Mark, Emily, Caroline, Ashley, Molly, and of course Colby.

Thank you will never be enough but I hope I love you is.

Dedication

This book is dedicated to my Lord and Savior Jesus Christ. Lord I am so thankful for your unyielding acceptance. I offer this book as a form of worship and praise. I offer you my mind and my heart. In addition, I offer recognition to my late mother Daisy Allison. I would also like to shine a light on my two children who in spite of living with sickle cell disease has been a continuous inspiration in my life. Let us all grow in the favor and the glory of grace and knowledge through our Lord and Savior Jesus Christ. To him be all the glory.

MARVIE BOLAND

Acknowledgement

This book would not be possible without the support of my wonderful husband Busta, Honey I thank you for your Love, prayers and support.

To all my children Yvonne, Lewis, Richard, Christopher, Johnathan, and Kyrene Marie, I love you all so very much, Words cannot express how much you all mean to me, To all my grand children, "I LOVE YOU" and my three beautiful daughter-in law, Tameka, Brendie and Simone, thank you for your love.

To the ones that pushed me to pursue my Passion: Shelly Gowan, Paula Singer and Debbie Bluestein.

Last but not least to Pastor Joanna Birchett of Gospel 4 U Network, my publisher, Thank you for all the hard work.

Introduction

THE CREATION OF MOM'S WINDS: DAISY ALLISON

My mother Daisy Allison was a beautiful spirit. As a Jamaican woman she believed that everything in nature possessed a life force. She always taught her children to judge those that would presume to be good and even those that had an inclination to be bad, according to how they treated us. Naturally favoring the ones who kept her children from wrath, of course. She believed in the interconnection of her spiritual beliefs, rituals, and daily life. Mother's law, as I call it, declared thusly, "My children, those of you who can keep strong, do good, and stay in God's will, will one day make it into a real human being." Please remember that my mother was from the islands and spoke as such. But what she was saying succinctly, was that we are not worthy to be called human beings if we can't do right and live according to God's laws. The apostle Paul said God's *"law is holy, and the commandment holy and just and good"* as well as *"spiritual"* (Romans 7:12, 14).

King David wrote, *"The law of the LORD is perfect, converting the soul,"* and he went on to describe the beauty and benefits of God's testimonies, statutes, commandments and judgments; as well as, various aspects of biblical law (Psalm 19:7-11). Our souls are converted into being counted worthy as we steadfastly strive to obey the law of the Lord.

Mother would say, "Remember baby girl, He makes no mistakes; His power knows no bounds." And I believe that through God's everlasting love and mercy, you can grow. One of my fondest childhood memories is when I used to gather berries with my mom. She taught me how to properly prepare different food for the upcoming winter. Her voice was so beautiful and her magical melodies carried in the wind. I can hear her voice now. And I'm thankful that her voice has stayed with me because when my mother grew ill, I would remember her teachings and be grateful that she instilled a strong foundation within me.

Her body had started succumbing to cancer and I believe that after a discussion had taken place in Heaven, God and His angels decided to spread out their wings and the cancer enveloped my mother's body. Cancer touched my mother's body and the effects reached down to her very soul. My mother Daisy Allison fought the good fight against these hellish monsters that claimed her physical form for as long as she could. God decided to intervene and His plans to call her home came to pass. She was wrapped up in a beautiful blanket of light in all her beauty and strength when she went home to our Lord. Like a cloud passes in the wind, like a swift arrow to heaven she was carried away. The angels rejoiced that this beautiful woman had reached them safely. A place where cancer can be no more. To my mother, no words could ever express the depths of my love and gratitude for you. The following scriptures comfort me daily, knowing that my mother is no longer in pain.

Revelations 21:3-5

3) And I heard a loud voice from the throne saying: "Behold, the dwelling place of God is with man, and He will live with them. They will be His people, and God Himself will be with them as their God. 4) He will wipe away every tear from their eyes, and there will be no more death or mourning or crying or pain, for the former things have passed away." 5) And the One seated on the throne said, "Behold, I make all things new." Then He said, "Write this down, for these words are faithful and true."

CHAPTER 1

A GRANDMOTHER'S TOUCH

WAKE UP! As your ears listen to the voice of this West Indian girl who never would have opened up her heart to anyone in the past. As you read the pages of this book you will begin to see how fortunate she is and to hear what the little voice echoes in the wind.

I have considered as my underlying theme in this volume; the way of a little girl from Jamaica. I have considered that the way of life that I, the little girl from Jamaica enjoyed, was directly related to my spiritual beliefs and the rituals of my daily life. I believed that everything in nature possessed a life. All of my mother, Daisy Allison's children, believe this. We believe that the sky, earth, mountains, trees, waters, animals, birds and man possess life in their respective forms. My mother believed and taught us to believe, that all rain or hail came from God. We believed this so much so to the extent that I learned and have discovered that even the sky contains its own special spirits within.

Ephesians 6:12/ King James Version (KJV)

[12] For we wrestle not against flesh and blood, but against principalities, against powers, against the rulers of the darkness of this world, against spiritual wickedness in high places.

The sky has a song that is only for God's sensitive

ears. As we learn from the aforementioned scripture, our challenges really come from the sky. The sky contains the principalities, powers, rulers of the darkness of this world and winds. And God endeavors to tell us of things to come by the way the elements in the sky move and the way the winds blow. I believe that every wind that goes forth in the earth has been breathed from the mouth of God. We can't see them but they are going forth in their spirit form and we feel them. God makes the winds blow far away and near, and they have their own special names. Let us refer to the book of Revelations.

Revelations 7:1 ~ *After this I saw four angels standing at the four corners of the earth, holding back the four winds of the earth, that no wind might blow on earth or sea or against any tree.*

I believe that God knows each of these winds by name and if you listen close enough you can hear their voice when they move and blow across the earth. Why do I believe this? Because everything has a spirit and therefore, everything has a voice. We can never again talk to our loved ones when they transcend into the heavenly realm but I think that sometimes we are allowed to hear their voices, containing special messages. I sometimes hear my mom's voice in the wind. I can still hear her voice. Sometimes I can even hear her sigh. I hear every whisper, bluster, roar, moan, and sometime whistle of her voice.

As it were, I was considering what the underlying theme in my mother's volume would be. And I have concluded that the way her spirit life impacted her children and in fact dwells in all her children is a testament to the strong Jamaican mother that she was and the eternal values she has instilled in us. Her life and her spiritual beliefs were related and the rituals of her daily life kept her connected to God's Holy Spirit. The Holy Spirit strengthened her spirit and the spirit within her was able to connect to everything around her, even the sky. The earth still feels her winds even though she no longer physically dwells on earth. The earth still feels the impact of her power due to her spirit life and her love for her children. One lesson, I've taken from my mother is that we who are still living are called dwelling spirits because we still dwell on the earth. Dwelling spirits can control nature itself. We, her children and grandchildren really believe that we can control nature itself.

Again, there are good and bad spirits that exist in mankind. The answer to which of those are good or bad can be determined by their behavior. She always told us to judge good or bad according to how they treated us; naturally favoring those that protected us from wrath or evil. And I don't know where my mother received her advanced knowledge but my mother also believed that angered spirits caused crop danger. There are evil spirits and in life all evil spirits associate themselves with darkness because those that are loose actually reside in deep underground caverns. They have emerged and do emerge periodically to perform horrendous deeds on dark forests. She would always caution that these evil spirits could cause us, her children, to lose their way home forever. These words and teachings would always cause me to pray harder whenever I traveled from my Jamaica to the northwest of the USA.

CHAPTER 2

VOICES IN THE WIND

Now I will give you another law as it relates to creation. Mom would tell me how when a person focuses on getting strong and keeping their strength and staying in the good will of the Father, that they will one day make it into becoming a real human being. A real human being has the ability to breathe into the atmosphere and create life. A real man or woman of God should always speak life. **Proverbs 18:20,21** says it this way; *20) With the fruit of a man's mouth his stomach will be satisfied; He will be* *satisfied with the product of his lips. 2) 1Death and life are in the power of the tongue.*

I don't say certain things because the power of life and death remains in my tongue. I'd rather take it to God and pray. I've learned even more so lately, that He's the only one who can fight my battles, comfort me, be my confidant, and will love me without conditions and so much more.

Therefore, be careful what you are creating but by all means, go out and create today. Go to each part of the earth and yield your breath into the atmosphere, wake it up. Go to other human beings near and far and breathe into them. Wake them up. There will be a human being with your breath, meaning that speaks *your* language and walk under a similar anointing, give that person half of your power and tell them what to do with it. Reader, today I am your power. I am transferring my power to you right now.

Some of you are like me. Some of you are speaking with the same breath that I do. I submit my power unto and into you right now.

"I would have it only as I am good", mom would say. I heard this in the wind as I listened for my mother's voice. "Baby girl a power just like me and God will help you do your work. Soon, even the creature earns their right to be a creature and so it goes for all their children. And you have made it into a human being. It is my duty to keep you all as peaceful as I can. When you have finished your work trust me we will meet again, not in this land but in heaven. And that is why I am speaking to you to remind you all to be good. Tell the truth and obey God. If you have done wrong someone else will make it where the wind blows them away to me. The mountain winds will rescue those who make fun of you. When you try to make the world a better place than you can meet the creator one day. Remember He does not make any mistakes; He has much power. He will also give you a second chance to change and He will take you to a great place that you may grow.

CHAPTER 3

PEACE, LOVE & NATURE

What happens when an animal wake into a person? What I'm explaining is that I used to feel like I was an animal. My introduction to this earth was not as a baby, it was as a baby animal. My spirit was so repressed and I was treated so inhumanely that I literally felt at times as if I were more animal than human. When a person wakes up and feels like they have beaver flesh you know that there is something wrong. At times I would have bigger revelations than others whereas I felt like I was waking up and becoming a brand new human being. And I would snap out of my animal mind and ask myself what do I suppose to eat? I know this seems hard to believe this is how I felt, because I was the Cinderella of the family and I would be left in the house to work and fend for myself. And the whole time nobody knew that I was going crazy and had almost lost my natural born mind.

See, I was introduced as a baby animal person, if that makes sense. Here are my roots, my mother would take me out and point out the bitter roots thawing and I would have to go pick them. She would teach me to cook them and how to preserve them in the freezer and other things about them that I did not know about. She would take me home and then start pointing out to me cherry bushes and huckle berry bushes, to service them. We'd pick them, she would cook and eat them. She would then show me how to dry them for the coming winter we were about to face. Am I still a new animal? By the grace of God, I have evolved into a full pledge human being. I love my mother and would never change my past because it made me who I am today. In my mind I would pray to the creator and say, "Lord, take me new places to see". And the creator would view the pictures in my mind and I can tell you today that I have lived to see those places. Every image that I painted in my mind, God has allowed me to see. That's me, from the beginning. I started from the pictures of rainbows that I used to see on the paintings of my mom. When I didn't have natural food, the things that I learned and seen from my mother was my food.

MARVIE BOLAND

CHAPTER 4

LISTENING IN THE SILENCE

Your ears can get used to the silence when you're in silence for a long time. When I was a little girl, I would wake up early in the morning and I would lie there and just listen. My ears would get use to the silence and it would focus on the voice of my mother. One Sunday, very early in the morning, I could hear my mom singing in the kitchen. The song would always begin very soft and low. It would then lift sharply to a high note and then fade gently away.

WHEN MY WORLD WAS VERY YOUNG

My mother was a beautiful, one of a kind woman. Daisy Allison was the one who got me ready for my journey into the new country, which was for me at the time, the United States of America. All young children as young creatures have huge appetites to devour everything. I was no exception. I wanted to learn to be transformed in my mind and soul and fly like a raven that I could obtain a strong mind that would allow me to speak with a loud voice instead of tears. I will not go head first in my dreams.

I could transform one dream into the next. I would make up my mind to live in my new land and behold, I would be there. I would eat and drink to my heart's content in the dream. And these would be of a spiritual nature sometimes and at other times it would be experiences of the mind. These experiences shaped me as a young girl.

I would never change my life on "land" for many

reasons. I will love the new people and I will not be like a "tough wood" that makes rough wedges in other people's life. Yes, don't get me wrong, I have grown tough and strong and I will need many, slender, straight shoots. But God will give me white blossoms, like the kind that is seen in early spring, to bloom in many people's lives, as they come my way. I would want people to say that I am like soft wood from the cedar trees and that my bark is from the roots of the same tree. I would ask God not to give me dry heat, but instead to make me good wood for kindling. I want God spruce my heat up in all ways when I get old and to allow me to finally be worthy of the title human being.

MARVIE BOLAND

CHAPTER 5

PAINT MY LIFE WITH BRIGHT COLORS AND BEAUTIFUL PEOPLE

I want to be a raven, so that I could perform my magic so quickly that no one can see what was happening until things are firmly in place. Because I don't ever want to be a trickster raven. I never want to destroy the world that I love so much. A world where the rains are formed in the sky high above and falls down on us. And the rain falls down on the many because many people share this world. Which teaches us that no one is better than the next person because the rain falls on the just and the unjust. Consider the text:

Matthew 5:44-48

44) But I tell you, love your enemies and pray for those who persecute you, 45) that you may be sons of your Father in heaven. He causes His sun to rise on the evil and the good, and sends rain on the righteous and the unrighteous. 46) If you love those who love you, what reward will you get? Do not even tax collectors do the same?

Have you ever wondered or considered the fact that all of us have a monster in us, and if we don't kill the enemy in us that we've been in a sleep –like state the whole time? Many of you are laying there waiting for the baby monster to kill you. Many of us have coyote like spirits that have killed the monsters in us and removed the bitterroot from its mouth and ask God to let it be. I always stand like a tall rock stands, so that I can't be touched by the monsters that would ravage me if they could. Jesus is the rock I stand. All other ground is sinking sand. How about you reader what is the rock that you're standing on? Is it high enough?

So wake up, those of you who have been slumbering, and get back to the rock.

Psalms 18:2-3

2) The LORD is my rock and my fortress and my deliverer, My God, my rock, in whom I take refuge; My shield and the horn of my salvation, my stronghold. 3) I call upon the LORD, who is worthy to be praised, and I am saved from my enemies.

You will feel the storm coming and you will see the rock coming towards you. If the rock comes to you from the mountains, then you should understand that our God has answered and has heard you. Cry (Amen) somebody! Lift the dead rock and let it fall and be crushed and then go out to the mountain, which is more like the rock that we're supposed to stand on, and go to sleep.

CHAPTER 6

WHY ARE YOU SO UNHAPPY THAT YOU ARE CRYING?

God made so much land for us to run around, but sometimes it feels like the earth is, for lack of a better word, sleeping. The reason why is because we have kept Jesus Christ from reigning on the earth. Jesus is no longer in the plains and in the fields. Jesus is no longer in the lakes and the rivers. The water is draining off the earth, the land is drying up, and these are not symbols of good these are symbols of famine. So we find ourselves crying more, to see if we could drop more tears to cover the earth with water again.

Many people are unhappy because of these situations and there are too many of us that are too busy to notice. There are many lonely people in the world because we do not have time to visit with them and we wonder why the mountains are crying. They cry when they look down and see the land drying up and all the land is saying bring it back to me. And the mountains are saying bring it back to me. And the mountains are saying bring my beauty back to me then I won't be sleepy. So the earth speaks out to the mountains and say I will lie down for a while and when I wake up I will run swiftly and move with haste to return back to my former glory.

I do not know what I want totally but I have made up my mind that I will have fun with the earth while I am here. Nevertheless, God gave me vision one day. When I looked up to the mountain there was young people talking. They were not getting into any trouble, they were laughing. They were not running and hiding from police and from guns, they were peaceful and content. The beauty of the vision is that I know few young people that are not naturally happy and it is not normal for them to habitually cry; so I was encouraged. Soon, I will sit down and dry a few more tears so that the mountain do not have to do a job that it wasn't created for and drop water on the land anymore. The only water that will be necessary will only come from the sky.

MARVIE BOLAND

CHAPTER 7

COLD WIND HAD THE POWER TO RULE

Do you know that if you take a bath in cold water that it will make you strong like a tree with strong roots that is set on a hill? There is something about the sound of the tree on the hill when the winds are blowing. Oh how I miss the sound. Mom would show us the difference between the warm wind and the cold wind. She said that the cold wind had the power to rule, it let you keep boulders for many miles and she always want us be like more like the warm wind, to be the strongest people in the world, to give love, and believe in God. The cold wind has been given the power to rule because of the fall of man and sin, but we should be more like the warm and gentle wind of God.

Do not take revenge and always be ready to help people, she would say. She told us the good that we should do unto others before the sunset and before the day was over, and said that we should never be like the cold wind. Have you ever heard the term, giving someone the cold shoulder? That is exactly what we are not supposed to do, be, or represent. Be the warm wind and we will always be stronger and the humans that embrace this wind will always be the strongest in the world. God never wants us to be like the cold wind because cold wind people throws water on ice hoping to make it slick but the warm wind people throw hot broth on the ice to melt it because it is rough and hard to traverse. So this is how we defeat the cold wind people and the warm wind people are continually and daily set free by the power of God, because God always makes a way for them. But the interesting thing that I've observed since I was a little girl is that the cold people could never find their way back and hence, became defeated in their own ice age, so to speak, of their own creation.

The Power behind Granted Wishes

2 years ago, sickness came upon my mom, who lived in the country of the United States of America. I almost died but so many people died that it seemed as if the whole family and subsequently nation would soon pass away. There is no medicine greater than God's power, because He is the great chief above us. My mom wants to say this to my 2 siblings a month apart. She says tell my family that I will send a message to them on the day after the moon is full, gather all my children together at the wishing well and tell them I am free. I am not sick no more, the medicine man sent out runners on the morning 3-

19-2014; all were dressed in their best robe. And please understand that there were no sick people with them.

Mom floated into Heaven right in the view of Jesus Christ, as the sun reached toward the heavens and all of His angels' eyes looked where He pointed; they saw a light and they saw a figure appear in the sky as they watched. They saw that the figure was a woman floating beautifully toward them. Her one wish was granted, as she was sent to her children. She was coming down slowly from the sky and rested on us, her children's shoulders, then spoke to us and said, "Please gather around me." Mom said this to her children, "Ask the great above what you will, because God has heard your cry and your prayers and He has sent me and the angels to help you my children. Do not cry or be worried about me because we are all healed here. And I have been healed from my sickness. We are crowded here and there is no sadness or sickness here." So we all shouted with happiness. She lifted her hands and hugged us saying, "I will not come again anymore. Now you must do what I tell you all to do. You must plant a seed that I shall give you. It is camas seed. Plant it everywhere. In the spring, it will have blue flowers and there will be so many of them. They will look like a blue lake. In the fall, gather the roots and you will remember that I no longer have cancer. Now I will be going home to heaven. I will have caught up with the breeze and carried back to the sky. My children, you can watch until I can no longer be seen among the clouds and I will send out a sign; and it will read. Mom of the camas. Meaning my sickness will never return. This is my gift that I have left for you my children."

MARVIE BOLAND

CHAPTER 8

BUSTA: BACKBONE OF THE FAMILY

I got married a long time ago to a man from the island of Jamaica. One day he decided that he wanted the girl next door for his wife, but he knew better than to ask for her. Then he thought he would wait until later. So, during the day he sat around becoming better acquainted with the family, specifically, my grandmother and grandfather. He was very neat and I noticed that he looked very strong. My grandparents talked between themselves wondering if he would be good for their granddaughter. One day, my grandfather said that we should go up to the house and give him something to eat. However, because it was getting late and it was only a few hours before sunset, we invited him to eat with supper with us instead.

My grandparent roasted beef and everyone sat down to eat the wonderful meal. My grandparent asked him how did he like his supper, he replied to them that this wasn't a meal it was a feast; and he asked, "Is this the kind of food you eat every day?" It was truly a wonderful occasion. My grandparents then asked him "Why are you visiting us and what do you want to ask us young man?" He answered, "Well it is like this, I would like to marry your granddaughter." said Busta. Both of my grandparents looked at each other but said nothing, Busta went for a little walk to allow the grandparents to talk privately. While Busta was gone my grandfather asked my grand mom, "What do you do think about this fellow? If we let him marry our granddaughter maybe they will stay here. But if not, perhaps some other young man, not as good as this fellow, will come and ask us for our granddaughter." Soon Busta returned and he decided to let my grandfather lead the conversation. My grandfather held his pipe in one hand and said something to the effect of how he wished that he had a smoke because his tobacco had run out sometime ago. After a while my grandfather spoke, "My wife and I have talked over your proposal and she and I have come to the decision to let you marry Marvie. We also will allow you to live here and then when you're ready to go away you will be able to take her with you." "You need not worry", said Busta. My grandparents were pleased with Busta and believed what he said so Busta took their pretty granddaughter, me, for his wife and he became the backbone of our lives. All of this happened in 1972.

THE GREAT POWER ABOVE ANGRY

When I came to this country in 1972, we entered the

United States of America at a place called The Mount Hood. There is also a place called Mount Adams. Mt. Adams stands closer to the USA than Jamaica. Mount Adams, I would call Jamaica, Mount Hood, I would call the United States of America. They both stood on the south bank between the two peaks of Cuba, where the big rocks formed an arch between the waters of a great sea that flowed peacefully until it got to a certain point. That point was the rocks of Miami. The peaceful waters turned dangerous at the rocks called Miami. Some people admired the big arch over their heads and were proud of the great power above that made other people afraid. Some traveled the dark journey to the south and their lives was not peaceful. The mountain did not let the blacks remain at peace. The Bible says in **Ephesians 6:12 (KJV)**

12) For we wrestle not against flesh and blood, but against principalities, against powers, against the rulers of the darkness of this world, against spiritual wickedness

in high places.

There was a powerful spirit and the spirits were jealous of each other. Each was proud of its beautiful home and each envied the beauty and grandeur of the other. Sometimes they become so jealous and so angry that they threw some rope on our ship and tried to stop us. Some even boarded ships and went to Africa for us. The great power above was made unhappy by their frequent quarrels and they let them fight until they grew weary of fighting. Mount Hood instead became friends and stayed at peace. The spirits became more and more quarrelsome with each other; they become more and more angry. They shook the earth in the Southwest between Mount Hood where we peacefully entered and came in as friends. Because fighting made the earth tremble, I took a long step and leaped over the island to my first mountain, the United States. In God I will trust.

MARVIE BOLAND

CHAPTER 9

RAVEN AND MY GRANDMOTHER

The island of Jamaica, West Indies is my native home. I lived with my grandmother. When I returned from the city to live in the country I became a raven. I remember taking on too many duties before and after school and sometime I would become so hungry. But I never begged for food, but when everyone would leave, the raven would come and take all the left overs. And the raven and her grandmother lived. But one day my mom called up the Great Chief, whose name is Jesus Christ. After she prayed, we waited. And one day the Chief let us see a little advertisement in the Jamaica Star looking for young girls to be a nanny in the state. She applied and waited. After a week or two, she announced with excitement that she was selected from all the rest of the girls to travel to the state for a short time. Hunger was forgotten as the girls lined up for their goodbyes. For a few moments, Raven, aka Marvie, aka me if you haven't figured it out yet reader, felt like I just wanted to take out a big bag and cry. I could hear my grandmother and other family members rejoicing as they drove away. However, before they left, my grandmother gave me a hug and said to me, "The Great Chief, Jesus Christ, will carry you over the big ocean and mountains and one day you will never hunger. Also, you will dress in their very best costumes and jewelry." About one year later, Raven, aka Marvie, flew away preceded my mom Daisy Allison.

When I arrived, I found a little house, filled with

love, maintained meticulously, and kept very neat. I could see that I was home. When the night would come however, Raven was cheerless and worried, due to leaving her grandmother. My mother would hear my cry and she would invite me to lay my head on her chest and seek rest in her arms. I would find peace and sleep in my mother's arms and would always wake up by myself finding that my mom had gone to work. I started remembering my grandmother smell. She smelled like an old straw bedding basket. I did not pay any attention to my Mom; however, I would remember grandmother's words. Those words were that obedience, respect, and love are essential. I now had plenty of food and beautiful clothes but I was still unhappy. I know now that I was just home sick. I became very lost within myself and the second night was the same, I just wanted to come alive and feel life. But, every day Raven would take a pebble of my grandmother's memory to comfort myself. Whatever reminded me of her, I would hold onto that. This process helped me to get better, and the pit that I found myself in, I slowly started climbing out it. In a few weeks, without a word, I found myself not feeling suffocated anymore. When this process reached its completion, Raven's new life in the new country finally began and now I have returned to my birth name, Marvie.

MARKED FOR TRANSFORMATION

I prepared myself with the help of God to move by His Spirit in the direction that He would have me to go. I asked God to allow me to put my feet on the right path and to allow me not to be moved. I asked Him to allow my choices to never again align me in the path of hunger. God answered me by showing me who I was for two years. I hunted for my purpose without luck for two years. Why? Because I could not see my face. I did not know what my God given mark was. One-day God told me that I had the power to find it. The next night I started reaching for it by praying when, all of a sudden, a light shone past my face. But that confused me. Then I heard a voice way down on the inside of me, and it asked me a question. It asked me, "What do you really want to say? There is someone on the inside of you that wishes to speak to you." However, under the circumstances, my mind was not clear. I did not want to fall into that kind of trap, where my mind was telling me only one thing; run away. But God blocked the way and said, "No, find your mark and then you will see that for years you tortured yourself, you burdened yourself, and put yourself in your current condition." "I demand you to take it back immediately, otherwise you will not find your mark," said the Lord. That day I was very cautious because I was going out too find me; and I was no longer frightened. With the help of God, I transformed myself, and I will never allow anything to disturb me from being me again. I found my mark. Please excuse me as I take a bow.

MARVIE BOLAND

CHAPTER 10

I AM THE WOMAN LIVING OVER THERE

Silence followed for some time after the initial experience of me finding myself. The second rock hit closer as I developed into a real woman. But I do not know what was the matter with me. There was so much whistling in my head when the many rocks came to hit me. I cried out with two sickle cell children and then a series of bad things started happening. I always had to run hot baths and ensure that all of the rooms were kept warm. When the summer weather kicked in, I had to keep it cool. Crisis kicked in and there were many emergency room visits. There was a time when they couldn't sleep to sound and I had to monitor that. There was always a strong wind ready to blow during that time. So I would have to hasten to them before the pain become too strong and the hunting started. The dawn would approach as I laid my head down. I could feel my heart rush to warn me. It would hurt me as I waited to hear if they were going to call out for mom. I would then feel like I had become a pain victim because of the extreme exhaustion that my body was feeling at that point. I would then tip my head for a quick 30-minute nap.

I feel like I can still feel my children's pain. While I would be going to get rest I would still have to tend to their every need. Sometimes after eating their food would come back up, but they were still not too tired go back to their own corner. I can still hear their little voices asking, "Can I have some breakfast in the morning Mom please? And can we have some Ensure, our favorite drink?" I believe that my kids were feeling like they were literally underground and they would only suddenly appear every time the killer pain would appear. I remember my son Christopher, around 15 years old, would cry out and the words and sounds that he was making was addressing the pain. The pain would seemingly respond. However, God would respond and say I don't want to kill you. But my son would reply to the pain and say that I am afraid you will kill me someday. The Lord would speak up again and say, I swear I will never try to hurt you, but my son would answer, why does my pain hurt and torment me so?

Every time I was about to fall asleep, he, the pain, moved closer to me and began talking to me keeping me awake the entire night. God replied, I am there am in control of your pain and you will notice in a few, that I will let you fall into a deep, deep, sleep. I am the Lord and you will notice that I can block the pain that has fallen on you. Because I will not let your pain, aka satan, carry away another corpse. I will stop the bow and arrow and kill it before it turns into anything substantial. As soon as your pain starts, I will shout directly to the pain, now you shall die. Please obey without questioning me.

GENTLE PUSH

Sometimes I feel like a great butterfly fluttered down from the clouds with a gentle push. I look around and I see that people are increasingly growing selfish and more quarrelsome and this behavior, in my opinion, is making the earth annoyed. The Holy Spirit wants me to warn you to be honest with one another and to live in peace from now on. Nevertheless, even as I give you this message, I am on notice that some of us will not want to and in fact will not heed this gentle push. Some will ignore this warning and will allow their evil ways to destroy them. Will you ignore this gentle push and allow your evil ways to destroy you?

Suddenly, there was a bright flash in the heavens.

The bright flash would soon be what we identify in today's terminology as a lightning bolt, and very loud thundering and roaring accompanied it from heaven. It was a signal for the great flood to begin. God can gently push if He wants to but the result of that would be that none of the bad people would be saved. However, I'm here to tell somebody that He will again, gently push, and He will send another flood. It will be a different kind of push and it will affect the good people and will be the beginning of the process that cause them to eventually live eternally with the Son of God.

MARVIE BOLAND

WORDS OF ENCOURAGEMENTS

MARVIE BOLAND

HOW WE SHOULD MOVE ON

When I was looking for a place that I could call my own to live, it was like I seen a light that got brighter and brighter. I watched people carefully I started to pick up the provisions that I would need to live in an abandoned shell of a house. I wanted people around me that was fun and full of life and so I greeted them all in a very friendly manner as if they were one of my own. I would give them beautiful turquoise from my own room. Those who wanted to move on I always wished them much happiness and a pleasant journey. Invariably, one day out of extreme curiosity, they would open the bag and look inside. After seeing what I gave them, they would rejoice.

MY CHILDREN FOOT PRINT

Do you ever feel overprotective regarding your children? Sometimes, when I'm trying to protect them, I feel as if there is a great giant with evil ways approaching them so quickly that I would like to dig a hole and hide them in it. I dearly love my six children and one day I thought I saw my children's footprints in dirt right near me and I laughed heavily and said, "Those are my hand prints?" My children that I will always love and support from the goodness of my heart. I will pray repeatedly regarding them covering them with God's grace. So much so that one day when they open their eyes, a beautiful rainbow will appear, creating a large bridge too cross into Heaven. My children names are Yvonne, Lewis, Richard, Christopher, Johnathan, and Kyrene-Marie.

SECOND SIGHT IN THIS AMERICAN WORLD

There is a difference between the world that I live in presently, compared to the world that I came from, if that makes sense. There were many questions regarding a colored woman in a strange town? I smile at these questions now. Because I am not interested in the questions, I am interested in reality.

See, I have a few questions myself. For instance, how does it feel to be considered a problem as a child to the point, where people would always wonder who you are? As I reflect back to my childhood, I believe that perhaps this revelation burst upon me all at one time. Because this was my childhood reality.

There was one day in particular, I remember it well, when the shadows swept over me. I was a young girl in the big world of the United States of America and the winter storm was raging and blowing extremely hard. Welcome to a new comer, the wind was saying. Then it dawned upon me with a certain suddenness, that I was different from everyone else. On the other hand, perhaps it was the veil that I applied over my heart, that I would use to shut me off from the world. The truth is that there was a vast veil that I applied for my protection, and I had no desire to tear down that veil for anything damaging to creep through.

THE WORKERS IN CHRIST VINEYARD

One day Marvie asked God a question. "Oh God could I just close my mind and lock it off from everything that was morbid and poisonous?" Sometimes I feel like this is my only vaccine against all the morbidity and poison in this world.

Poison has entered in the system. By system, I mean the system of humanity and the experience of life. I offer in this book a way to approach life. I sometime lay there at night. Not self- examining but shedding my daily garment of sin; whether of omission of commission. I believe that God forgives me and that every day I will wake up a free woman, with a new life, that I can look back on with no regrets.

THE HADICAPPED IN ME

Many days I feel like a handicap on the course of my life because of curses combined with the mistakes of yesterday. I, like most people, feel that some of my prior actions are paralyzing the efforts of my life today. The worries of the past hugged to my destruction and regret was allowed to canker the very heart of my life and when God allowed me to see this and matured me into a true woman this became something of the past. Whether past or future, I've learned to be content. The load of tomorrow added to that of yesterday only makes me stronger. Behold, I am a new creature, old things have passed away, I am a new woman who makes each day the epitome of life.

2 Corinthians 5:17 ~ *Therefore, if any man be in Christ, he is a new creature: old things are passed away; behold, all things are become new.*

MY GRANDMOM

Often I think about my grandmother. What was her childhood like? While she was raising me, I could see a little of her life in her words and actions, but not much. However, I can remember seeing how faithful and stringent she was concerning education. She strove to learn at all costs. She would very often be very weary. I used to notice how here and there her foot would slip and she would sometimes even fall. As I reflect, we must understand, that we should always look dimly at the past and don't focused on the things that we can over criticize regarding our journey. We should at least give leisure for reflection and change.

After my childhood, I suspected for the first time as I reflected and analyzed the burden of my Grand mom. She lived in poverty and sometimes she didn't have a cent to her name. She lived in a little mini house, but her mind and love for God was rich. She would say to be poor is hard, but when you find yourself in the place of poverty, remember one thing. "To have God and believe in Him makes you richer than a dollar bill." God will give you the correct blessings at His specific time. God's hands are quick. He will give you eyes to see, good and gifted minds, pure hearts and will free you to live beyond the measure of your strength. He who bears it in the name of Jesus, will always go through this world with good humor and grace.

Isaiah 65:17

For behold, I create new heavens and a new earth; And the former things will not be remembered or come to mind.

HATE

The very moment when every part of my being was raptured in the presence of God. Moreover, when every part of my physical and spiritual body began to speak to God, my enemy came nigh and I started fiercely praying in his face. My lips went as fast as my spirit could pray and my eyes became narrow as I turned the enemy away with the power of prayer.

The bitterness in my heart and vagueness in my soul, said to me the same day, that when this passes and when all the arrows that we possess are cast, we will ask one another why we have hate for one another and will fail to find a good answer. This is the mystery that I have regarding hate. I still wonder after we come to this level of realization, how can we still hate each other?

MARVIE'S PRISON WALL

Jesus suddenly seemed too real as the sky above my head became like a cascade of scorching steel and I felt, or thought maybe is the better word, that my soul was in pain. The pain that I had I can't explain it, but only to say it was as if I was being hunted. I quickened my steps as I tried to run away from something like an eye that was trying to kill my family.

I love my family but I still had to let it be heard. It made me unhappy to unload on them but with each of them I had to be heard so do it with love. Some does these things with a bitter look, some with flattening words, but the one who don't have the guts at all doesn't do it and I would call a coward. A coward is just like Judas; with a kiss. But I was brave and I shouted, I hate you all. I tried to kill all of their love and some never got over it. Some things were still left in me when I got older. Because some people have taken my kindness for weakness and have gently put a knife in my back.

I always give too much love. Some love too little and then some love too long. Some sell for love and others buy love. I give with love accompanied with many deeds. The prison wall was surrounding me; an outcast girl, abused by the world because the things that I trusted in was used to hurt me to the heart. But God, from His endless reservoir of care, removed the iron bars that I put around me. I never knew that the dripping wall was so high. It was when Jesus light shined on the wall beneath the ladder in the sky, that at last I saw the shadowed prison bars. The prison bars shuddered and shocked. The prison clock and all of the jail bars, that seemed so important to me before, were in despair. And then I knew that my white rose had started to bloom right while I was in my prison. I could smell the flower even through the prison air. It would heal me and strip me from my prison clothes. Because God always see's the good in me, He will never leave me nor forsake me. I was with child and my eyes and my body watched through my prison walls as the Son of God looked upon me. Now I am free. What a mighty God I serve no more prison wall in me.

MENTAL AND PHYSICAL TRAINING

Do you remember that most touching of all incidents in Christ's ministry? It was when the rich ruler named Nicodemus came to Jesus by night. He was worried less about the things that pertained to his every day life. Because of the ministry of Jesus, He worried less about the things to his busy life. He became more concerned regarding things that pertained to his everlasting peace. Christ message to the world back then is never more needed then at the present. We must be born of the Holy Spirit.

We should be the leaders of men, spiritually. We should make known the great soul that has set in place the morals of the world. We must be born of God's Spirit and initiated into the fraternity, so to speak. I always want to begin the day with Christ. And I choose to refuse the literature of the world to learn and know my bible. As my grandmother, grandfather, and mother has done before me, I want to continue in these traditions. These things form your character and shapes your conduct.

I have also learned that the quiet life is made up of compartmentalized day time increments so that the night time will not have any power over you. I want to help you to beat your own burdens reader. With a light heart to all generations, I want to be remembered as a strong woman into whose life you've entered by reading this book. I hope that my words have provided inspiration. I pray that my words will help some of you to number your days so that you may apply your hearts unto wisdom. My message is but a word, a way, an easy expression of my experience of a plain woman whose life has never been guided by any philosophy higher than that of the Good Shepherd. My purpose is to point out a path in which women will not forget to adopt good habits. The practice of living is to be practiced and I have allowed the depth of some of my feelings to be expressed in this body of work. I am a woman that in my opinion, started life in the best of all environments, a parsonage, as one of 7 children.

JOURNEY IN SEARCH

For Adam and Eve, time started with their expulsion from the garden. It started with the opening of a door. But for Marvie, it started at the moment in which the unthinking and timeless innocence of my childhood took on the many dramatic turns that I've written about in this body of work.

We all have moments in life, or have had a series of moments, but one way or another the journey through time started for us. The journey starts for all of us one way or another. For some it starts when we're searching for the start of that moment. I will end my journey with faith, hope, and love. The names of the three that will carry Marvie through time to lighten my steps as I go is set and I will never question the truth of what I fail to understand. For the world is filled with wonder. And in the long run, nothing, not the world or Heaven myself can separate us for an eternity. My journey shall continue.

THE CREATION AND THE FALL

The Bible begins with the words; God said let there be light and there we saw that the light was produced in order for people to escape from a naïve fundamental literalism. We see the creative hand of God bringing energy into being in the creation of the first atom.

RESURRECTION

John 20:28-30

28) Thomas replied, "My Lord and my God!" 29) Jesus said to him, "Because you have seen Me, you have believed; blessed are those who have not seen, and yet have believed." 30) Jesus performed many other signs in the presence of His disciples, which are not written in this book.

THE CHURCH TRIUMPHANT

Eden Restored

Revelations 22:1-5

1) Then the angel showed me the river of the water of life, as clear as crystal, flowing from the throne of God and of the Lamb 2) down the middle of the great street of the city. On each side of the river stood the tree of life, bearing twelve crops of fruit, yielding its fruit every month. And the leaves of the tree are for the healing of the nations. 3) No longer will there be any curse. The throne of God and of the Lamb will be in the city, and his servants will serve him. 4) They will see his face, and his name will be on their foreheads. 5) There will be no more night. They will not need the light of a lamp or the light of the sun, for the Lord God will give them light. And they will reign for ever and ever.

The church becomes the church triumphant here. We have a glimpse into the heavens whose multitude no man can number. We see the city of God, whose lamp is the lamp and whose light lights up the whole world. The nations walk the river of life that is clear as crystal, as it flows from the throne of the Lamb which has taken the place of the old the old temple.

I choose to end this body of work with these images. The death of someone you love is a serious thing. It is something so huge that it takes time to grasp the reality as a fact. Even when it is grasped it is so overwhelming that it cannot be held on to for a very long time. It comes and goes as the spirit struggles and fails to keep it on the perimeter of consciousness. As you can tell this body of work was motivated by mother Daisy Allison's departure into God's Glory over two years ago. My mother's death, in a way, was a beginning for me and until eternity ends I will honor her memory and wisdom that she instilled in me and in this earth. May God bless everyone who reads these pages.

DAILY DECLARATIONS

MARVIE BOLAND

DECLARATION

O Lord, who hast taught us that all of our doing, done without charity, isn't worth a thing. Send thy Holy Spirit and pour into our hearts that most excellent gift of charity. That whosoever lives in you is counted dead before Thee; wherein when we are dead to self we are alive in you. Grant this God's only begotten Son.

In the name of Jesus Christ, Amen.

Daily Prayer for Love

Thou shalt love the Lord thy God and thy neighbor as thyself. Love cannot be contained. When you add to the love of God by treating your neighbor, as you want to be treated and then go further by loving your enemies; it pleases God. Yet, obviously, we do not, or the world would not be in the state that it is today. We do not love vividly enough. Love is strong enough to allow us to avoid conflict, especially for those who seriously desire to get along with one another and settle disputes. Love brings resolution, because when the power of love is applied, powerful healing takes place, quickening takes place, and the enduring bond of peace is manifested that surpasses all understanding. Moreover, all of the virtues are from God Himself. He who comes to do good knocks at the gate. He who love finds the door open. Love that includes warmth, interest, unselfishness, and a desire for another's welfare and growth.

DECLARATION

O Lord I know not what I ought to ask for from thee. Only thou know what I need. You love me better than I know and you love me more than I love myself. I simply behold my need; which I know not nor can I see. Raise me up Oh Lord, as I stay silent. I offer myself and my desire to thee, to accomplish thy will. Teach me to pray for more of you in me. There are many ways to pray and each soul must find its own way. The important and essential thing is to pray. When I first started praying, I prayed in disbelief until I got to a later stage of spiritual maturity. I did not feel anything in the beginning other than a void that was indispensable to my body. So your prayer is indispensable for the soul. I am not a woman of learning but I humbly claim to be a woman of prayer.

I am in different form when I am in prayer. The only way

to pray is to pray and the amount to pray is as much as you can. It is a good thing to give thanks unto the Lord and to sing praises unto thy name. *O Most High to tell of thy loving kindness early in the morning and of thy truth in the night seaso*n **(Psalm 92:1:2).** Our first thought in the morning and our last thought at night should be of God. Whether we ear press it as the psalmist plays on an instrument or whether in the secret recesses of our hearts. in the twilight period between being asleep and being awake.

ABOUT THE AUTHOR

Marvie Boland is a woman that wears many hats, she is the CEO and founder of *"Bows Passion of Fashion."* A fashion designing and Interior Decorating company, located in Pennsylvania and Georgia.

Marvie has a passion for children, so she has designed a special clothing line for Children under Bows designs.

Check out a few of her *"BOWS"* designs on the next pages. To contact her feel free to visit her website at www.bowspassionoffashion.com

MARVIE BOLAND

BREAKING THE SILENCE & SHOUTING FOR JOY

DESIGNER, DECORATER AND FASHIONABLE

MARVIE BOLAND

www.ingramcontent.com/pod-product-compliance
Lightning Source LLC
Chambersburg PA
CBHW071153090426
42736CB00012B/2314